Clouds Of Inspiration
Photos And Poems

Dwayne Cole

Dedication

This book is warmly dedicated to all lovers of clouds. Clouds can take on mysterious colors and shapes. Walking in the beauty of Alaska in the last decade, I've watched in awe as clouds morphed into hearts, gods of myth, and Jonah's whale. With their infinite changeability and untouchable height, it's no wonder clouds have been given mythological and folkloric qualities by many cultures.

I breathed this prayer for all cloud lovers—

Spirit blow as a gentle breeze
inspiring us to soar in the clouds,
high as the heavens,
new horizons to explore.

Contents

Dedication 2
Introduction 5
Clouds 7
Flying Saucer Clouds 11
Wisdom of Unknowing 13
Heart Cloud of Hope 14
Clouds of Inspiration 18
Waterfall Wonder 21
Beauty in Clouds 23
Seeking a Golden Cloud Haven 24
Snow Dance 28
These are the times that try our soul— 29
God's Home 31
Magic Purple Cloud 33
Sunlight expresses something that is more than human. .. 35
Seeing/Being 47
Rainbow Promises 57
Rainbow of Hope 58
Rainbow Surprise 59
Celestial Rainbows 59
Rainbow Turns Trees Magical 61
Celestial Rainbows 66
Nature Haiku by Granddaughter, Clara Thomas 69
Views from breakfast table in Hawaii 74
Clouds of Inspiration 81
Heaven and Earth Become One 85
Arrayed in Wonder 86
Ten Reasons to Observe Clouds 87
Cloud Watching 88
The Dawn 94
Concluding Poems 95
In the Clouds 96
Clouds 98
Clouds of Inspiration 102
Other Books By Dwayne Cole 103

Introduction

"No matter where the people traveled, God was with them. Each day a cloud was over them to guide them, and each night a fire could be seen in the cloud."—Exodus 40:38

Jesus took his disciples into a high mountain where his face was shining like a bright sun. From a cloud a voice said, "This is my own dear Son, listen to what he says." —Matthew 17:5

Clouds can stir the imagination. These puffs of air laced with water crystals take on mysterious colors and shapes. it's no wonder clouds have been given mythological and folkloric qualities by many cultures.

In the Bible clouds are symbols of God's presence and guidance. The people were inspired to lift their eyes to heaven and walk in faith.

In ancient Greek myth, clouds were seen as a group of young nymphs called Nephelai. These cloud spirits, depicted as beautiful and transparent, spent their days collecting water from the rivers in cloudy pitchers, then floating up to the heavens to pour water down from the sky, nourishing the earth and feeding the streams. Nephelai sailed through the sky in billowing white robes, looking like swans.

Hindu tradition reflects the belief that elephants brought the rain, and that clouds themselves were the celestial relatives of the white elephants that roamed the earth. An elephant's body was thought to be representative of a cloud, and they would use their trunks to shower the earth with rain.

Native Americans also created myths and folklore around clouds. Some saw clouds as the clothing of the gods of heaven. A god spreading arms would cause the clouds to move across the sky.

Even today, cloud myths endure, often associated with honoring the dead. The Pueblo, an agricultural people, believe that the dead become the Cloud People and send them rain, thereby nourishing their land.

There's no doubt about it— There's just something about clouds that is utterly magical. And it's not just you and I that have that feeling. It's a universal phenomenon throughout history.

Clouds

I love to watch the clouds.
See them rise above the snow covered peaks.
See them come like a flock of sheep
skiing down mountain trails.
Roll into cotton candy ropes
In the valleys below.
Kneel at the altar like bride and groom.
Above the blue waters
turn into a humpback whale,
and bounce along the waves.

The Chugach mountains
with great pride, taking selfies—
Shine, shine on all!

No matter where the people traveled, God was with them.
Each day a cloud was over them to guide them,
and each night a fire could be seen in the cloud.—Exodus 40:38

Flying Saucer Clouds

Glory forming from water crystals
Swirling dervish of sun colors,
Cloud dancers gathering intermingling light
of yellow, gold, gray, and purple delight.

Swaying, spinning
their way across the sky.
Dance into the mystery.
Soul arrayed in wonder.
Eyes lifted to heaven's glory.

This journey is not for mortals.
On this dance one is swept
into a flying saucer cloud—
Flying to realms unknown,
the realm of celestial seraphim!

Poetry is the dream
that brought the first morning
Shines with the brightness of a new day
Twinkles in every cloud
Purity of fresh waters
Swims in salmon spawning
Nature lifts our spirits

Wisdom of Unknowing

The only true wisdom is
in knowing you know nothing.—Socrates

Wisdom
I studied her

I became burdened
With knowledge of her

Then I went silently into
A glorious sunrise

A golden spirit sings
Without words

Astounded by sermon in clouds
I stood naked and speechless

Insight came
In wisdom of unknowing

Clouds of unknowing
Came to me.

Sunrise wisdom
Is more than human

Wisdom of the Saints
Filled me.

A golden heaven
Sings for everybody

Heart Cloud of Hope

A daughter picks up
a picture of her parents

Floats into a heart cloud
Two hearts enfolded as one

Memories of love
Trickle down her cheeks

Memories now entwined
In COVID-19 realities—

In the fields spring lilies will blossom
Opening star-studded hands

Ethereal Beauty
Heart cloud of love beckons

Family felicity.
Hope springs eternal!

(Written on 12-15-2020 for the families who had lost loved ones in the pandemic— over 500,000 had died from the corona virus just in the USA at that time).

This heart-shaped photo was taken in Alaska

while walking with my love of 56 years.

Standing behind two spruce trees,

holding hands and tickling fingers.

Swaying in the gentle breeze.

Our universe moves

toward inspiring beauty and wonder.

Nothing is more grand

than the union of two hearts—

Never to be apart.

One for Eternity!

Clouds smiling warmly,

welcoming the new daybreak.

Shine, shine, shine on me!

Watch me respond with kindness

and smile warmly on all I meet.

Clouds of Inspiration

Glory forming from water crystals
Swirling dervish of creative colors

Cloud dancers gathering
Intermingling sunlight

Yellow gold
Gray and purple delight

Birth of the universe
Spinning into existence

Swaying, streaming
Across the sky

Flying to realms unknown
New days of celestial seraphim!

We can speak without voice to the trees
and the clouds and the waves of the sea.
Without words they respond
through the rustling of leaves
and the moving of clouds
and the murmuring of the sea.—Paul Tillich

We can speak with a few carefully chosen words
Magical moments that nature sings without voice
Autumnal leaves whispering praise anthems
Clouds caressing Alpenglow mountain peaks

Without words nature sings magical tunes
Autumnal leaves whisper anthems of praise
Clouds caress Alpenglow mountain peaks
Bird wings flutter inspiring faith and hope!

    Chugach mountain peaks
     and sky kiss so shy
   Clouds wink blushing pink

Waterfall Wonder

A gurgling waterfall
Coming out of the clouds
Laughs on way to sea
Singing a joyful melody
Come bathe your soul and be free

Waterfall from the clouds
Clouds from the waterfall
Gulls come from both
Laughing, making music together
Orchestra playing as one

Sun rising at 10:25
As I walked into the park
Puffs of clouds catch fire
In awe my soul draws flame
My feet barely touched ground

Beauty in Clouds

I fell silent
when I saw from my rock pillow
the last sliver of the fiery sun
illuminating the radiant Chugach peaks.
In the glow Sol looked as though
she were stripping off all her clothes.
The clouds blushed their approval.
My heart fills with adoration!

Oh Beauty in the clouds.
On the mountains turned golden.
A beauty that has called to me
through all my years
In tadpoles and Mill Rock streams.
With faith, hope, and love
With deep soul joy
and heartfelt delight.

Seeking a Golden Cloud Haven

Sitting on my deck
watching the sun
gild the mountain peaks.

The wise raven of Alaskan lore
soars into view.

I've seen this before
in fact, many times,
but it is never ho hum.

An always fresh scene

from the artist's palette,
a sneak view of one peak

in the 250 mile Chugach range
running through Alaska.
I snapped the picture.

When I viewed the scene
I saw that I had captured
the raven of Alaskan myth,

tilting, leaning,
into the
updraft of warm air,

etching a black y
in the golden-eye
sunset sky.

Speed an obvious joy.
The vibration of air
around its flattened

pennaceous
plumulaceous
feathers

whispers
a faithful prayer
of gratitude.

Seeing.
Sensing.
My soul, seeking a haven

from the world's craven,
pusillanimous ways,
joins in the prayer.

The way the raven
looked down at me,
a gleam from a golden sky,

sent my spirit
soaring in the clouds
saved for eternity.

If this is not prayer
from a raven,
a wise maven,

I don't know what is!

(I try not to use big words that might cause the reader to stop and wonder the meaning, maybe look up. Since this poem is about the wise raven, maven, I thought it appropriate to use a few new words and watch raven wink. This poem is taken from my book, Alpenglow Miracles: Fire Dance of Wonder).

Snow Dance

Chugach winter rehearsal
Birch trees dancing in bronze britches
Pink clouds blush approval

These are the times that try our soul—

Nations experiencing fatigue

Storm clouds darken

Grow more threatening

Souls tested

On deck praying again

In response to yearning

Great Artist of the universe

Becomes a passionate flame

Paints a radiant Alpenglow sky

Clouds catch fire

My soul draws flame

Hope springs eternal

Kindness is like a beautiful stained glass window
that gathers the light of heaven
and warms all in its glow.

God's Home

I am poverty. I am solitude.
I renounced spirituality to find God
Who preaches loudly beside the running waters.
—Thomas Merton

While the man-made

church houses are closed

Go into God's home

the world of nature

Dreamed and crafted by angel's hands

You will find God's birds and flowers

preaching joyful goodness and love

Butterflies and bees singing anthems of praise

In a sanctuary where kindness

is the stained glass windows

greater than the Sistine Chapel ceiling

painted by Michelangelo

Nature's Alpenglow clouds

gather the light of heaven's dome

Shine on all God's creatures

The doors to this chapel

are always open

The grassy sod is the plush carpet

Welcome mat inviting all to worship

Magic Purple Cloud

In the mystical land of the far North
where Santa and his magical elves live
colors are spectacular

The Northern Lights, Aurora Borealis,
can fill the skies with ribbons of
blue, red, purple, green, and yellow

Magical alpenglow colors transform
mountains, clouds, and trees
into beautiful works of art

In this magical light, digital cameras,
especially in automatic mode,
love choosing the color purple

Snowshoe dancing in morning light
taking on aura of purplish haze
leaps into mysterious magical realm

My snowshoe friend,
take me with you—
Let me dance into mystery!

(Photos taken in early sunrise with misty rain. Red sunlight shining through blue clouds gave snowshoe hare a purplish tint and created the magical purple haze.)

Sunlight expresses something that is more than human.

A family member asked me
to share some wisdom
for these times of pandemic.

In seminary I studied wisdom.
Learned to read Hebrew, Greek,
French, German, and a splash of Latin.

Drawing on my command of words,
I will say nothing!

Dogs teach us that sometimes
 it is best to just turn around three times
 and lie down for a long nap.

ZZZZZZZZZZZZZZZZZ

I woke with the question
bouncing up and down the corridors of my soul—
O wisdom where are you hiding?

As I often do, I went for a walk
and witnessed the sunrise.
I stood speechless.

A golden spirit sings to me
without words.
Astounded I stood naked
and speechless.

Insight came
in wisdom of unknowing.

Clouds of unknowing
came to me.

Wisdom of the Saints
filled me.

Sunrise wisdom
is more than human knowing.

A golden heaven
sings for everyone!

A common daily phrase is "I need a lift." It can mean I need a ride. However, it more often means, "I need a caffeine lift." Or, "I need my coffee." I doubt you have ever said, "I need an orographic lift." Living in Alaska along the 250 mile Chugach mountain range, I often lift my eyes unto the hills and say, WOW! Here is why.

What looks like a snow covered mountain in the background is actually a cloud formation called orographic, from two Greek words---oros (mountain) and grapho (write). Orographic is best translated as writing mountain shaped clouds. The warmer air rising around the mountain encounters cooler air and condenses into water vapors that are formed into the shape of the mountain. They can be seen rising along the 250 mile Chugach range and rapidly dispersing as they rise higher.

As a student of the Bible, I am familiar with the importance of clouds in God's good creation. Clouds are often the means of God's direction and a rising of hope. In the central Old Testament story of the Exodus, God directs the people of God on their journey to the promised land by going before them in a cloud. In the new exodus delivered by Jesus in the New Testament story of the cross and resurrection, Jesus is lifted into heaven by a cloud. And we find this phrase in the New Testament---all of God's people are under the cloud, meaning under God's goodness, grace, and mercy.

> Rows and rows of clouds.
> Send rain and snow on everyone.
> Love notes from heaven.
>
> Saying, "I love you."
> Inspiring our lives with joy.
> Singing every day.

I walk into a beautiful rainbow.
Face the deep fears of pandemic.

Felt I was not of this time and place.
Gazed and waited.

Then Nature's Beauty looked back at me.
I became one with the visible universe.

One with heaven's blue canopy over me.
Security, Promise, and Hope within me.

Ascended into higher realms unknown.
Awakened by Beauty and Grace.

Emboldened by nature's tender touch—
The strength of Oneness!

Began to see with new eyes—
All my fears and pain were drawn
into the heart of Kindness.

Overcome with Goodness and Mercy!

The unbounded Joy
of being kissed by a Lover—
Dancing in a new day.

Finding one's name written
in the shining clouds.

The gift is buried treasure.
Hope in Beauty and Wonder!

(Photo used in my book, *God and Evil: An Ode to Kindness*)

Sun slowly sinking,
painting mountain and clouds pink.
Bedroom all aglow!

View across Cook Inlet of Mount Redoubt,
an active volcano in South West Alaska that last erupted
in 2009. It is over 10,197 feet tall.

Beth and I look toward the mountain
Here since mountains began

Draped in glistening snow
Blanketed in silver clouds

We feel so small
Shoulders slump

From the weight
of the suffering world

The mountain says to us
I was born out of volcanic eruptions

Pushed up into the heavens
Touching the One who carries

The weight of the whole world
The One feeling our pain

Out of pain
Comes new birth

Our spirits rise into clouds
Becoming two gulls

Soaring in the heavens!

Twilight revelations

All is not eternal night

Clouds shimmer golden

Mountains become luminous

Silence turns lament to praise

Seeing/Being

Lift the wizard's wand
Heaven comes down

Trembling verdant leaves frame
billowing clouds and snowy peaks

Revealing new relational ways
of seeing and being

Viewing pastoral scene
Embracing Beauty and Wonder

Experiencing soul-quakes
Tenderly feeling goodness and love

I listened quietly
to the music in my heart

Bringing to light the soul of nature
Transforms the inner undiscovered self

Lips wet with Muse's nectar
Joyfully sing Alleluia!

The mountains writing
orographic clouds today
shape shifting miracles

62 degrees and blue skies
with warm air rising
drawing moisture
from the snow and ice

As they rise
clouds are shaped like the mountains
thus orographics—Two Greek words
oros (mountain) and grapho (write)

Watch the shape shifting miracles
Experience soul-quakes

Let me be lifted into the glow
Let my life write
Messages of faith hope love

In Greek mythology, Nephele (Νεφέλη)
was a cloud nymph.
In biblical faith stories,
God leads people in a cloud.

In this nighttime photo,
taken from our condo bedroom,
Nephele is reclining for the night.
Her face becomes the face of God.

As Sol sinks in the western sky,
pink shades are drawn.
From high above—
The full moon comes to sing a lullaby.

Language of words is inadequate
to capture the magic moments.
Loved ones smile from above
in these transformative times.

Fathers, mothers,
Grandfathers, grandmothers
are near when heaven and earth
become one reality.

Many hearts joined in love
become One—
One becomes Many in time,
Many become One in eternity.

Be still, oh my soul!
Rest In peace.
Wrapped in love.
Free from fear!

After a morning of snow clouds,
covering the mountains in secrecy,
the veil was lifted. Revealing visionary blue skies
wrapping the mountains in mystery—
Covered with fresh snow,
sparkling with celestial glee,
singing in the breeze.

Rainbow archery
God's radiant clouds of care
Promises of security

Rainbow Promises

I walk into a beautiful rainbow.
Face the deep fears of pandemic.

Felt I was not of this time and place.
Gazed and waited.

Then Nature's Beauty looked back at me.
I became one with the visible universe.

One with heaven's blue canopy over me.
Security, Promise, and Hope within me.

Ascended into higher realms unknown.
Awakened by Beauty and Grace.

All my fears and pain were drawn
into rainbow promises.

Rainbow of Hope

I have great faith
in kindness
Brought by rainbows

Faith in deep yearnings
of the soul
not yet fulfilled

See rainbows
Slow down
Take off shoes

Listen
Remember
Forgive

Breathe deep
Recover from fears
Heal

Hope
Wrapped
in goodness

Rainbow Surprise

Walk in Chugach
Revealed

Easter egg
prize

Mountain glazed
Rainbow

Reaching
Bluebird sky

Heaven to earth
Uniting

Celestial Rainbows

Sometimes the whole world
is a rainbow painted
with angel wings.

Radiating love energy.
Opening new dimensions of
promise, security, and hope.

Gifts from the celestial realm!

Rainbow Turns Trees Magical

My six brothers and six sisters and I
grew up loving trees.
Three brothers and four sisters have died.
I often think of them
residing now in heaven along with mother and daddy.

When Herbert and C. E. were teens
they especially liked trees.
They got the idea
to tie an old iron framed cot
high in a walnut tree.

After a hard morning
of plowing mules in corn rows,
they would eat a quick lunch,
climb in the walnut tree,
take a bow.
tip their cap,
and lie down for a nap.

Seeing this tree and mountain
wrapped in a rainbow
I took a bow,
and said, thank you,
brothers and sisters,
mother and daddy,
for visiting me.

Were they in the tree top?
If elves dwell in trees
and angels descend on Jacob's ladder,
my family can slide down heaven's rainbow
and sit a spell.

I know this:
Seeing this tree aglow
with shimmering incandescence,
wrapped in a rainbow,

I sure felt their presence!

Ocean working hard
to compete with golden skies
Splash clouds along beach.

Sometimes the whole sky
is a rainbow of color—
Beauty to inspire!
Bedroom drapes are open wide.
Night-time clouds are blushing pink!

Celestial Rainbows

Sometimes the whole world
is a rainbow
painted with angel wings.

I wish I could create for you a rainbow
Shining with all the colors of heaven.
And let it shine in your soul.

So each new day would radiate
love energy from the rainbow
opening new dimensions of
promise, security, and hope.

But that is God's miraculous work!
Gift from the celestial realm!

I love pancake flat
Lenticular alpenglow clouds
Over Alaska mountains

Ribbons of delight
Blinking like coy eyebrows
Through bedroom windows

The clouds catch fire
to give glory to God's name.
Let my life do the same!

Nature Haiku by Granddaughter, Clara Thomas

Mountains shoot the clouds
Tall and proud Denali stands
Birds fly by mountain

The Yukon flows proud
Goes through Alaska to sea
Salmon jump for joy

The trees stand so proud
Spruce, cottonwood, and willow
Trees bend low in wind

In Autumn leaves fall
Gold, red, orange, and yellow
Winter comes so near

When your world is upside down
Stand on your head.

The trees will grow out of the ground,
and the clouds will billow overhead.

Photo taken by my friend, G. W. Reid

I stand under golden trees
gazing into the pale blue sky
consumed by cirrus clouds.

I look into the blue waters
and see the same scene.
Am I gazing up or down?

The trees, the sky, and the lake
are all one in nature's array.
In witnessing the scene,

I am one with nature's beauty
one in goodness,
one in life's grand family.

The face of God
is seen in the lenticular Alpenglow clouds
stacking like pancakes over the mountains.

Yet, do we see the gleam on the human face
shining greater than ten-trillion stars,
and draw closer as the image of God?

Climb high in the birch tree.
Sit quietly.
Become
one of the limbs.

Listen to the music
of the trembling leaves.
Feel soul-quakes.

Watch the cirrus clouds swim by.
Big as whales in the blue sea sky.
One could do worse
than be a climber of birch trees!

Views from breakfast table in Hawaii

The daystar having completed
its westward run,
passes the glowing baton
to a shivering silver moon.
Having won another victory,
rises to turn the clouds golden.
Promising a bright new day.

Quiet contemplation
Gazing at the silent clouds
Hear angels singing

See what great beauty
Can clothe our lives in wonder
Resurrection mirth

In Greek mythology, Nephele (Νεφέλη)
was a cloud nymph.
In biblical faith stories,
God leads the children of God in a cloud.

In this photo from last night,
taken from my condo bedroom,
Nephele is reclining for the night.
Her face becomes the face of God.

As Sol sinks in the western sky,
pink shades are drawn.
From high above—
The full moon comes to sing a lullaby.

Language of words is inadequate
to capture the magic moments.
Loved ones smile from above
in these transformative times.

Fathers, mothers,
Grandfathers, grandmothers
are near when heaven and earth
become one reality.

Many hearts joined in love
become One—
One becomes many in time,
many become One in eternity.

Be still, oh my soul!
Rest In Peace.
Wrapped in love.
Free from fear

Chugach mountain peaks
Become peppermint candy
Trees beam golden smiles

Sky and mountains kiss
ever so coy and shy
Clouds wink blushing pink

Clouds are poems written in the sky
Only God can make a cloud
God is the Supreme Poet

Clouds of Inspiration

Glory forming from water crystals
Swirling dervish of creative colors

Cloud dancers gathering
Intermingling sunlight

Yellow gold
Gray and purple delight

Birth of the universe
Spinning into existence

Swaying, streaming
Across the sky

Flying to realms unknown
New days of celestial seraphim!

Poetry captures the dream

that brought the first morning

Shines with brightness in each new day

Wraps love in clouds

Twinkles in every star

Purity of fresh waters

Swims in salmon spawning streams

Nature lifts our spirits

Heaven and Earth Become One

World turns and changes
Lays down a golden road
Heavens beamed praise
We are invited to change
Join chorus of alleluia

Fortune telling sunrise
Transforms gypsy journey clouds
Into heaven's angels

Arrayed in Wonder

I wake to a sun-magic world
Captivating beauty
Arrayed in wonder

On the artist palette I see
The blending of earthly
and spiritual light

Travel along fast flowing streams
Cascading down
from rivers of glaciers

Seeking to find myself
in the eternal entanglements
of appearance and reality

Summer silver birch trees
Shadowed into child's toys
by the looming scale of rising mountains

In grasping the shadows
the poet finds substance
The essence of the universe

Drawn into the mystifying scene
Glory and dream merge
I find my place in the cosmos

Contemplating in nature, I see a Nurturing God of love,
patiently, giving value to all things. Inviting and
      empowering us
to join in this adventure. Persons nurtured in nature are
compassionate, empathetic, and always caring for others.

Ten Reasons to Observe Clouds

1. Clouds are a source of wonder and awe in many religions and especially in the Bible.

2. Clouds are associated with two of the central events in the Bible: the exodus of the people of God from bondage in Egypt and the resurrection and ascension of Jesus.

3. Observing clouds today can wrap one in the mystery of miraculous actions of God.

4. The beauty of clouds is like floral bouquets that speak of God's beauty and love for us.

5. Clouds contain and provide life sustaining water by bringing showers of blessings to us.

6. Clouds are universal and spark global consciousness of all things being connected in nature and in faith.

7. Focusing on the beauty and wonder of clouds, help to be more focused on the big picture, the spinning universe.

8. Clouds bring messages from unknown realms, bringing unknown to known, infinite to finite.

9. Cloud watching increases social activity, creating new friends.

10. The unique role of clouds in God's good world can inspire us to care for one another and for the only world we have.

Cloud Watching

I like to spend some time each week cloud watching.
Clouds are an important metaphor in the Bible.
In the central exodus story of the Old Testament, God
used clouds to guide God's people from slavery
to the promised land of blessing. In the New Testament,
Jesus, after his resurrection, was lifted into heaven by a cloud. P
aul, the Apostle, observed that all of God's people are under the
cloud. For Paul this means under God's care and will.
So, when I meditate under the clouds I have this biblical usage
of clouds in mind. I pray for all who have lost their way and live
in fear and doubt. I pray for God's will to be revealed
and God's strength to be sufficient for all of our needs.
This is my prayer for you.

> "The light in Alaska in particular
> is so beautiful. So beautiful!
> Such incredible light."
> —Sebastiao Salgado

Far in Alaska,
foothills of the Chugach,
a grandfather caring for his family
found solace and tender love.

Alpenglow-ology was born—
sunrises and sunsets said,
"Photograph me,
write a poem about me."

Immense loveliness
shining through nature
brings mornings full of joy
and evenings so glorious-wild.

The mountains and skies,
the sun, moon, and stars,
the alpenglow clouds,
each a miracle of love.

Wisdom comes
in the sun magic world
in taking the gifts that are given—
Beauty, truth, goodness, and kindness.

The Dawn

I like to sit on my deck
Quietly contemplating

Watch the Alpenglow clouds
on the Chugach range

Songbirds flutter down to trees
Leaves whispering soul music

Another world becomes visible
Possibilities wide and timeless

Dreams grown dim
Sing with new inspiration

I believe in the dawn
A grandchild's smile

Concluding Poems

Celebrate life with everyone
The star dust in my life is in yours
We breathe the same air
Belong to each other

The sun dressed in blue skies
With ruffles of silvery clouds
Shines on everyone
Great or small, rich or poor

See God in everything
Yet do not say you understand the Eternal One
God's thoughts are not our thoughts
Our ways are not God's way

The still small voice
Speaks in sunshine and dark clouds
In you and me

Linked together as one
Let us walk into the unknown
Unknowing all we have known
Learning a new language of kindness

I walk in nature to see with new eyes
To listen to the still small voice
Unknowing all that I have known
Learning a new language of kindness
Mother moose nuzzling new born twins

In the Clouds

All of my photos,
books, and poems
are in the iCloud.

All of my life
seems to be moving
toward the clouds.

Hope entwined in the web
with fear.

Wisdom
with ignorance.

When my biography is written,
let me be lifted
to an alpenglow cloud like these.

Enclosed in goodness.
Where I can smile down tenderly
on my family and loved ones eternally!

But please wait a little longer,
my story is not finished.
I have more work to do.
Let beauty glimmer through.

I want to show more kindness
on this side of the cloud.
Here grandchildren are watching me
compose my poems of loving kindness.
I have poems within me they have not yet heard!

Clouds

The fluffy clouds of God's morning sky quickly fade and fly.
I love those marvelous drifting clouds.

I saw this almost perfect orographic cloud formation as I got out of the car at our condo in Anchorage. Before I could get my camera ready for the picture, Zeus, the god of clouds, rain, and thunder blew on the orographic formation and lifted the top off like it was whipped cream. I stood there in awe watching it rise.

I breathed this prayer:
Spirit blow as a gentle breeze
dispelling my clouds of despair.
These early clouds of morning inspire me
to soar, high as the heavens,
new horizons to explore.

Golden dreams arise
On clouds up to heaven float
Gaining angel wings

Clouds blazing as fire

Light shines in darkness
Light we cannot always see
Yet eternally do

Clouds of Inspiration

Kindness gathers light
Heaven's life giving rays
Warms all in its glow

Each day is splendid
Shinning with new light of day
Angels voices hoarse

Oh what a vision!
At heaven's door, sky is red.
Heaven's gifts descend

A knock at the door
Must lift the latch from within
Christ is risen!

Other Books By Dwayne Cole

A Center that Holds: Adventures in Kindness
Alpenglow Miracles: Fire Dance of Wonder
A Prayer of Blessing: As You Go Remember This
A Relational Hermeneutic of Kindness
A Relational Trinity of Kindness
BEARS AND MOOSE OF ALASKA: Nature Poetry
Down on the Farm in Georgia: A Poetic Memoir
Dragonfly Magic
Gentle Galilean Glories: The Tender Teachings of Jesus
God and Evil: An Ode to Kindness
Jesus' Transforming Beatitudes: Selected Sermons from Year A
Jesus' Transforming Love: Selected Sermons from Year B
Jesus' Transforming Gentle Teachings: Selected Sermons from Year C
Kindness Is Every Step
Poems Inspired by Process Philosophy
Poet of the Universe: A Vision of Beauty and Goodness.
The Apostles' Creed: A Living Creed for the Living Church
The Book of Revelation: Jesus' Kindness Transforms Suffering
The Serenity Prayer: A Pathway to Peace and Happiness
The Story of the Bible: Authority, Inspiration, Canonization, and Translation
TREES AND DRIFTWOOD: Poetic Ecology
WINGS OF INSPIRATION

Clouds Of Inspiration: Photos And Poems
ISBN: Softcover 978-1-955581-44-8
Copyright © 2021 by Dwayne Cole

All rights reserved. No part of this book may be reproduced or transmitted in any form or by any means, electronic or mechanical, including photocopying, recording, or by any information storage and retrieval system, without permission in writing from the publisher.

Parson's Porch Books is an imprint of Parson's Porch & Company (PP&C) in Cleveland, Tennessee. PP&C is an innovative organization which raises money by publishing books of noted authors, representing all genres. Its face and voice is **David Russell Tullock** (dtullock@parsonsporch.com).

Parson's Porch & Company *turns books into bread & milk* by sharing its profits with the poor.

www.parsonsporch.com

www.ingramcontent.com/pod-product-compliance
Lightning Source LLC
Chambersburg PA
CBHW061201070526
44579CB00009B/93